Original title:
Holding My Own

Copyright © 2024 Swan Charm
All rights reserved.

Author: Liisi Lendorav
ISBN HARDBACK: 978-9916-89-712-6
ISBN PAPERBACK: 978-9916-89-713-3
ISBN EBOOK: 978-9916-89-714-0

The Light That Guides Me Home

In shadows deep, I seek the flame,
A beacon bright, calling my name,
Through trials fierce, I find my way,
With faith as my compass, I shall stay.

Amidst the storm, when hope feels lost,
I cling to love, no matter the cost,
Each whispered prayer, a soothing balm,
In the sacred silence, I find calm.

Your wisdom shines, a guiding star,
No distance too great, no journey too far,
With every step, Your presence near,
In every heartbeat, I feel no fear.

Paths may twist, and darkness loom,
Yet in my heart, Your promise blooms,
A light that nourishes my soul's deep need,
With every moment, I'm filled with creed.

So onward I walk, through night and day,
With gratitude, I trust Your way,
For in the heart of each wandering roam,
I find my way back, the Light that guides me home.

The Dusk That Holds the Dawn

In the hush of evening's grace,
Soft whispers fill the air,
Clouds part to reveal the space,
Where hope awaits with care.

Faint stars begin to glow,
Guiding hearts through night,
Promises that gently flow,
Turn darkness into light.

The twilight holds a dream,
In shadows, faith will stand,
As rivers weave a stream,
With each touch of God's hand.

So cling to the gentle night,
For dawn shall surely rise,
A symphony of light,
Where morning's peace complies.

In the dusk we find our way,
As hearts remain secure,
For every end gives way,
To a dawn that will endure.

The Promise of Tomorrow

Each day a gift unfolds,
Wrapped in warmth and grace,
A tale of love retold,
In every time and place.

Beneath the skies so vast,
Hope is stitched with care,
A future that is cast,
With faith beyond compare.

Moments blend and weave,
A tapestry of light,
In the heart, we believe,
Tomorrow brings its might.

Through trials we may roam,
In shadows, we confide,
For every step brings home,
The promise we abide.

So lift your eyes with trust,
To the morn's gentle glow,
Where all that's true and just,
Will guide us as we go.

Faith's Anchor in the Storm

When waves crash high and wild,
And fears begin to rise,
Remember, you are a child,
Of the One who hears your sighs.

In tumult, find your peace,
As anchors hold you fast,
Let every worry cease,
In love's embrace, steadfast.

The storm may roar and howl,
Yet courage blooms within,
Through trials, hear love's call,
A new day will begin.

In shadows cast by doubt,
Keep faith's light aglow,
For storms are but a route,
To strength we come to know.

So when the torrents swell,
And chaos fills the day,
Hold tight to what is well,
For faith will lead the way.

The Radiant Path of Endurance

With each step on the way,
Through valleys deep and wide,
We find the strength to stay,
With grace as our guide.

The road may twist and turn,
With trials all around,
Yet in our hearts will burn,
A light that knows no bound.

In moments of despair,
When hope seems far away,
A promise lingers there,
To lead us through the fray.

For every mountain tall,
And river deep we cross,
Will teach us through it all,
The beauty born of loss.

So walk with gentle faith,
And nurture love inside,
For on this path of grace,
Our souls shall safely glide.

The Garden of Self-Belief

In the quiet of my mind,
Seeds of hope I plant anew,
With each prayer, a gentle wind,
Nurtures dreams that will break through.

Faith like sunlight on the ground,
Casts away the shadows deep,
In this sacred space I've found,
Joy and strength begin to seep.

Weeds of doubt may try to cling,
Yet my heart will tend with care,
In this garden, I will sing,
Songs of courage, love, and prayer.

Each blossom tells a story true,
Of trials faced and mountains moved,
With petals soft and skies so blue,
My spirit thrives, my path approved.

In this realm of self-belief,
Contentment blooms, the soul set free,
With every sigh, I find relief,
And trust in all that's meant to be.

Spirit in Full Bloom

Awake, my spirit, rise with grace,
The dawn has come to light my way,
In every step, I find my place,
Through trials faced, I learn to stay.

Each moment sings of sweet delight,
In every breath, the sacred dwells,
As petals open, hearts take flight,
In love's embrace, the spirit swells.

With colors bright, my joy unfolds,
Where shadows fade, and laughter reigns,
In this garden, life consoles,
And beauty flows like gentle rains.

Awake, dear soul, to endless skies,
With faith as strong as rivers flow,
In every sunset, wisdom lies,
The spirit blooms, the heart will grow.

In unity, let us rejoice,
With every heartbeat, we are free,
In harmony, we find our voice,
Together in this sacred plea.

A Testament of Tenacity

Through trials fierce, my heart remains,
The strength within begins to rise,
Each challenge met, though frail the chains,
Defiance sparkles in my eyes.

In moments dark, my spirit learns,
With every stumble, wisdom blooms,
Through storms I weather, courage yearns,
In every shadow, light resumes.

Patience wraps my weary soul,
While faith ignites a fire bright,
Each step I take, I find my goal,
In every struggle shines the light.

Resilience woven strong and true,
In tapestry of hope I weave,
With every prayer, I start anew,
A testament, I will believe.

So here I stand, unbroken still,
With heart aflame and spirit high,
In every challenge, I fulfill,
A testament to never die.

The Altar of My Soul

At this altar, I humbly kneel,
With dreams and fears laid at Your feet,
In silent prayer, my heart will feel,
The sacred bond where we shall meet.

With every tear, a spark ignites,
In moments raw, I'm made aware,
Through shadows cast by endless nights,
I find the strength to bear my care.

In gratitude, my voice ascends,
Each whisper echoes, soft and clear,
As love transcends, the spirit mends,
Embraced by grace, I draw you near.

This altar holds my hopes and pain,
Where faith and trust entwine as one,
In every loss, a gentle gain,
A journey shared; the race now won.

So here, dear God, I place my all,
In reverence for the love I hold,
In every rise, in every fall,
My soul's rich stories yet untold.

A Sanctuary Within

In quiet whispers, peace will flow,
A sacred space, where stillness grows.
The light within, a guiding star,
In solitude, we find who we are.

With faith as roots, our hearts expand,
In gentle strength, we take a stand.
The shelter here, where love unites,
A refuge formed through endless nights.

Each tear that fell, a drop of grace,
Will carve our paths, and time embrace.
In moments small, the Spirit speaks,
A love that thrives, when hope seems weak.

So let us tread on holy ground,
In every heartbeat, truth is found.
This sanctuary, forever free,
A home for souls, eternally.

Harmony of the Heart

In gentle dance, our spirits sway,
The rhythm soft, leads us astray.
Each note a prayer, a sacred song,
In harmony, we all belong.

The world unites in colors bright,
Each voice a spark, igniting light.
With every breath, a chance to share,
The love that flows, it fills the air.

Through trials faced, we rise as one,
In every battle, love is won.
A symphony of hearts so true,
In moments shared, we are renewed.

Together strong, we forge ahead,
With faith as armor, love is spread.
In unity, our spirits soar,
A harmony that will restore.

Guardian of My Spirit

Protector strong, in silence stands,
A watchful eye, with gentle hands.
In darkness deep, my soul you shield,
Through trials fierce, your love revealed.

With every breath, I feel your grace,
A whispered prayer, a warm embrace.
In quiet moments, still I find,
A faithful heart, forever kind.

You guide my steps, through storm and strife,
With every trial, you gift me life.
In sacred trust, I lay my way,
A guardian near, who will not sway.

In joyous peace, my spirit thrives,
Your timeless love, it never hides.
Embraced in light, I walk with you,
A bond unbroken, strong and true.

Embraced by the Divine

In every breath, I find the light,
A love so vast, it conquers night.
With open arms, I feel the grace,
In every challenge, I find my place.

The universe, it speaks to me,
In whispers sweet, in harmony.
A spirit vast, in every being,
The heartbeat strong, in all I'm seeing.

Embraced by faith, I stand anew,
In sacred trust, my spirit grew.
With every moment, I will rise,
To dance with life beneath the skies.

Together bound, in love's embrace,
In every trial, we find our space.
The divine spark that lights our way,
In unity, we will not stray.

Beacon of Inner Light

In the depths of the soul, a spark ignites,
Guiding the weary through darkest nights.
Faith like a lantern, it brightly glows,
Whispering love where the spirit flows.

With each gentle breath, serenity found,
In silence and prayer, the heart unbound.
Hope dances lightly on wings of grace,
Embracing the light in this sacred space.

When shadows encroach, our hearts align,
Through trials and storm, His love will shine.
Like a beacon aloft on the ocean's crest,
In His warm embrace, we find our rest.

Kindness in action, our purpose clear,
Echoes of mercy in all that we hear.
Together we rise, like the dawn's soft light,
Transformed by the warmth of His holy sight.

Let faith be the compass, our true guiding star,
Leading us home, no matter how far.
With hearts intertwined, we journey as one,
In the name of the Father, the Spirit, the Son.

The Strength of Solitude

In quiet reflection, the spirit is still,
Finding that peace in a world of will.
A sacred moment, just me and the Divine,
In solitude's grasp, His essence entwined.

The heart learns to listen, the soul begins to soar,
In the depths of silence, we discover more.
Each whisper of grace that cradles the mind,
Reveals the treasures that solitude finds.

In the stillness, hope rises like dawn,
The burdens diminish, the fears are withdrawn.
With faith as our anchor on this quiet sea,
We gather our strength, and we simply be.

Awareness awakens, the heart starts to sing,
In moments of stillness, we feel everything.
The beauty of silence, a soft, gentle kiss,
Nurturing souls in the depths of His bliss.

Through trials and doubt, we grow ever strong,
In solitude's embrace, we find where we belong.
With hands gently raised, in surrender we stand,
Finding strength in the silence, guided by His hand.

Graceful Endurance

In the face of the storms, we learn to endure,
With grace as our cloak, our hearts remain pure.
Each trial a teacher, each challenge a gift,
In the dance of the hard, our spirits uplift.

The road may be rugged, the journey unknown,
Yet with faith as our anchor, we're never alone.
Through valleys of shadows and mountains of pain,
In His strength, we rise, time and again.

With every step taken, we honor our plight,
Finding beauty in struggle, our hearts shining bright.
For the fire of life may twist and may bend,
But grace leads the way, our truest friend.

Together we gather, in love we abide,
Through the trials we face, in Him we confide.
Our stories interwoven in faith and in trust,
With grace as our guide, we rise from the dust.

With courage and hope, we march ever on,
In the shadow of struggle, we're never withdrawn.
For with each graceful step, we're learning to be,
The essence of love, unshackled and free.

In the Shadow of the Almighty

Underneath His wings, we find our true rest,
In the shadow of the Almighty, forever blessed.
With faith as our shield, we face each new day,
In His gentle embrace, we are guided away.

In trials unending, His strength is our song,
Through valleys of sorrow, we find where we belong.
With hope as our lantern, we light up the night,
Finding solace and courage in His holy light.

When fears try to conquer, we rise and believe,
In the warmth of His presence, our hearts will not grieve.
Each moment a gift, a divine interaction,
In the shadow of His love, we find our attraction.

With grace like a river, flowing endlessly wide,
We walk hand in hand, with Him as our guide.
In the quiet of prayer, our spirits are swayed,
In the shadow of the Almighty, our fears are allayed.

With gratitude flowing, our hearts open wide,
In His loving arms, we forever abide.
For in every heartbeat, His presence is near,
In the shadow of the Almighty, we conquer our fear.

Harvesting Inner Grace

In fields where shadows play,
We gather hopes, not fears.
The heart, a sacred space,
Nurtures love through tears.

With every whispered prayer,
Seeds of kindness grow clear.
In unity we share,
The blessings drawing near.

Beneath the sun's embrace,
We find strength in our plight.
Harvesting inner grace,
We rise to greet the light.

With gratitude we stand,
Hand in hand through the storm.
Trusting a guiding hand,
In faith, we find our form.

In peace, the world will meet,
The fruits of love we sow.
Together, we are fleet,
In harmony we grow.

The Temple of Resilience

In each heart lies a flame,
A beacon in the night.
Built on trust, not on shame,
A fortress of pure light.

Brick by brick, we ascend,
To heights that fear can't breach.
A sanctuary to mend,
Where dreams become our reach.

With every trial faced,
We fortify our core.
In silence, love embraced,
We open up the door.

Each stone tells a story,
Of battles fought and won.
In our shared glory,
Resilience is our sun.

Through storms, we still stand tall,
In grace, we find our way.
Together, none shall fall,
In this sacred ballet.

A Tapestry of Self-Belief

Each thread weaves a tale,
Of strength and gentle grace.
In colors that unveil,
The beauty we embrace.

From darkest night to dawn,
We dance with vibrant hues.
With every doubt withdrawn,
We craft our sacred views.

In patterns rare and bold,
We forge our destined path.
In warmth, our hearts unfold,
To love, we turn from wrath.

With faith as our design,
We stitch as one, not two.
With every moment shine,
In love, we find it true.

Together, we believe,
In unity's embrace.
In this tapestry, weave,
The threads of endless grace.

Rising from the Ashes of Doubt

From embers of despair,
We lift our gaze in trust.
With courage, we declare,
From ashes, rise we must.

Each scar tells of a fight,
Of shadows we have crossed.
In darkness, we find light,
No hope shall be lost.

In whispers filled with grace,
We seek the strength to soar.
In every trembling space,
We find what we adore.

Together, we transform,
In love, our spirits free.
In unity, we form,
A new reality.

With faith, we rise again,
Beyond the pain we knew.
Through struggles, we gain zen,
Our souls forever true.

Rising from the Ashes

From the depths of despair we rise,
Fires have burned but faith complies.
In the night where shadows creep,
Hope emerges from the deep.

With every wound, a story told,
In the silence, we find gold.
Cleansed by trials, hearts grow strong,
In the embrace where we belong.

Beauty found in broken things,
From the ashes, new life springs.
In surrender, we find our peace,
From the struggle, sweet release.

A phoenix born from grief and pain,
In the loss, our lives remain.
Through the storms, we stand as one,
In His light, we've just begun.

Each step forward, faith in hand,
Guided by a gentle band.
Rising up through skies of gray,
In His arms, we find our way.

In the Quiet of Faith

In the quiet, whispers sing,
Hope is found in everything.
A gentle breeze, a soft caress,
In solitude, we find our rest.

With every prayer, a heart's release,
In stillness lies our inner peace.
The world may roar, but we abide,
In faith's embrace, we do not hide.

Stars above in night's embrace,
Guide us toward eternal grace.
Each silent moment, sacred space,
In the quiet, we find His face.

Voices fade, distractions cease,
Our spirits soar, our doubts release.
In the calm, His love ignites,
Illuminating darkest nights.

So, in the quiet, let us dwell,
In trust profound, all will be well.
With hearts attuned and spirits bright,
In faith, we find our guiding light.

A Heart Anchored in Grace

In storms that toss, we hold on tight,
A heart anchored in divine light.
Through waves that crash and winds that roar,
Grace keeps us steady, evermore.

Each trial faced, a lesson learned,
In every heartache, love returned.
Strength from scars, a beacon bright,
In shadows deep, we find our sight.

With open arms, we find our way,
In moments dark, we choose to pray.
Forgiveness flows, a river wide,
With grace as guide, we will abide.

A gentle touch, a soothing balm,
In chaos, we find the calm.
With faith's embrace, our burdens share,
In unity, we stand and care.

As anchors hold in troubled seas,
So does His love, our hearts at ease.
In every trial, love's embrace,
We find our strength, a heart in grace.

The Armor of Belief

We wear the armor, strong and bright,
In battles fought, we seek the light.
With faith as shield, our spirits soar,
In trust we stand, forevermore.

Each promise made, a sword of truth,
In youthful hearts, and spirits smooth.
With every prayer, we forge the might,
In the darkness, we shine so bright.

The enemy may loom and grow,
But in our hearts, His love will flow.
With courage clad, we press on through,
In every challenge, our faith renew.

Armored souls in unity,
Together, we walk on destiny.
In moments fierce, we do not fear,
For Love is close and ever near.

So stand, dear souls, in purest grace,
Embrace the path, and run your race.
With armor strong and hearts that believe,
In His protection, we shall achieve.

In the Sanctuary of Self

In stillness, hearts do pray,
The light of peace, our guiding way.
Amidst the noise, a sacred space,
Where souls connect, in love's embrace.

In whispers soft, the truth is found,
A gentle grace, in silence bound.
Reflections deep, like waters clear,
In solitude, the spirit draws near.

With introspection, we seek the dawn,
Awakening the heart, reborn.
Through trials faced, we learn to rise,
In faith we trust, as hope complies.

The sanctuary, both vast and small,
Within our beings, it holds us all.
Where burdens fade, and joy takes flight,
In quiet corners, we find the light.

With gratitude, we lift our song,
In harmony, we all belong.
In the sanctuary, we find our peace,
In love divine, our souls release.

Embracing the Divine Within

In every breath, the spirit flows,
A sacred dance, where love bestows.
With open hearts, we welcome grace,
Each moment a divine embrace.

Awakening to the inner glow,
A sacred fire begins to grow.
In stillness found, we seek the truth,
In innocence, we find our youth.

With every step, the path unfolds,
The whispers sweet, the heart beholds.
In every tear, a lesson shared,
In every joy, the soul is bared.

Embracing light, we shine anew,
In unity, we find our view.
The sacred within, a holy space,
Where silence speaks of love's own face.

In every soul, the promise lies,
A spark of hope that never dies.
Together as one, we shall begin,
To cherish the divine within.

A Pilgrim's Solitude

In quiet paths, the pilgrim strides,
With faith as guide, the spirit glides.
Through valleys deep, and mountains tall,
In solitude, we heed the call.

With every step, the burdens fade,
In whispered prayer, our fears displayed.
In heart's reflection, truth is found,
In stillness wrapped, our souls unbound.

The journey weaves both joy and pain,
In every loss, a chance to gain.
Through tears of sorrow, we shall rise,
In pilgrimage, we seek the skies.

With open arms, we greet the dawn,
In nature's choir, our hearts are drawn.
With humble hearts, we walk the way,
In solitude, we learn to pray.

Each step we take, a sacred vow,
In faith we trust, in love we bow.
The pilgrim's path, though long and wide,
Leads to the light that cannot hide.

Shielded by Faith's Embrace

In trials faced, we find our strength,
With faith as shield, we go the length.
In darkest nights, a beacon burns,
A guiding light, through which heart yearns.

With every storm, we stand as one,
In faith's embrace, our race is run.
Through doubts and fears, we find our way,
In love's own arms, we choose to stay.

With fervent prayer, our voices rise,
In community, our spirits fly.
Together bound, we face the fight,
In faithful hearts, we find our might.

With gratitude, we lift our song,
In harmony, we all belong.
Shielded by love, we walk the line,
In faith's embrace, our souls align.

In every moment, peace bestowed,
As faith within, continues to grow.
Together we stand, strong and free,
In faith's embrace, our destiny.

The Inner Sanctuary

In silence deep, the soul shall rest,
A sacred space, where we are blessed.
With whispers soft, the Spirit calls,
In the heart's temple, love enthralls.

Within these walls, no shadow lies,
Light dances forth, through quiet sighs.
Each breath we take, a prayer ascends,
To seek the peace that never ends.

Here in this place, we find our truth,
In gentle grace, we drink from youth.
The world outside may clash and roar,
But in the heart, we seek no more.

The Inner Sanctuary holds our light,
Guiding our paths through darkest night.
With faith as shield, our spirits soar,
Embracing love forevermore.

So come, dear soul, and find your way,
In stillness profound, let hope convey.
The Inner Sanctuary welcomes all,
In sacred peace, we hear the call.

The Light of Truth Within

In every heart, a spark does glow,
A flicker bright, the path to know.
Amidst the trials, it shines so clear,
Guiding our steps, casting out fear.

The light of truth, our guiding star,
Illuminates the way from afar.
With every choice, in love we trust,
For in the light, our souls are just.

As candle flames in darkest night,
We gather strength, united in light.
With open hearts and hands laid bare,
We share the truth, beyond compare.

Let truth arise, dispelling doubt,
A river's flow, steadfast and stout.
In unity, we stand as one,
The light of truth shall never shun.

So seek it deep, the light within,
A beacon bright, where love begins.
With every breath, let it ignite,
The flame of hope, our endless light.

Eternal Flame of Resolve

With steadfast heart, we face the storm,
An eternal flame, steadfast and warm.
In trials faced, our spirits rise,
A light shall guide beneath the skies.

Through darkest hours, we find our strength,
In every challenge, we go the length.
With courage fierce, we stand our ground,
In faith, the victories are found.

The flame of resolve burns ever bright,
A beacon fierce in the silent night.
With every doubt cast to the side,
In unity, we boldly abide.

As seasons change and paths may twist,
This eternal flame, we cannot resist.
With hearts ablaze, we journey on,
In every setback, new hope is drawn.

So let it burn, this flame divine,
A symbol true, our hearts align.
In fellowship, we bravely strive,
Eternal flame, in love, we thrive.

Standing Firm in Faith

In storms that rage, we hold our ground,
With hearts entwined, in love abound.
Through trials fierce, our spirit's grace,
In faith, we find our sacred place.

With every step, on rocky shores,
We lift our eyes, through open doors.
In every challenge, courage grows,
Through faith unshaken, truth still flows.

Emboldened hearts, we rise as one,
Chasing the light, till day is done.
Standing firm, our bond is steel,
In every moment, love we feel.

With hands held high, we face the fall,
In unity, we heed the call.
Through every shadow, we stand bright,
In faith, we find our guiding light.

So let us march, though trials lay,
In unison, we'll find our way.
Standing firm, in faith's embrace,
Together strong, we seek His grace.

The Path of Unyielding Hope

In shadows deep, we seek the light,
With faith as our guide, we rise each night.
Through trials faced, our spirits soar,
For hope unyielding opens every door.

With whispered prayers, we find our peace,
A gentle strength that will not cease.
Each step we take, a sacred trust,
Our hearts ablaze, in love we must.

Around us grace, like sunlit streams,
In every challenge, we hold our dreams.
With hands held high, we dare to stand,
Together as one, a faithful band.

In valleys low, or mountains high,
We walk with courage, we do not shy.
For in our hearts, the promise glows,
Through darkest paths, the light still flows.

So let us walk this sacred trail,
With hope as our shield, we shall not fail.
The path ahead, adorned with light,
In unyielding hope, we find our might.

Nurtured by Grace

In morning's hush, where silence sings,
A gentle touch, our spirit clings.
With every breath, a gift we share,
Nurtured by grace, in loving care.

The warmth of faith, a radiant glow,
Through trials faced, our roots still grow.
In trusting hands, we find our way,
Beneath the sky, blessings will stay.

With open hearts, we seek to serve,
In kindness shared, we find our nerve.
Each act of love, a fragrant bloom,
In grace's garden, there's room for room.

As evening falls, we gather round,
In whispered prayers, our hopes are found.
Through every storm, our spirits remain,
Nurtured by grace, we shall not wane.

So let us lift our voices high,
In harmony, we'll touch the sky.
For in this bond, our souls entwine,
Forever blessed, in love divine.

The Covenant of Courage

In quiet vows, our hearts align,
A sacred pledge, both yours and mine.
With courage bold, we face the fray,
A covenant sealed, come what may.

Through trials fierce, we find our might,
In darkest hours, we seek the light.
With steadfast love, we stake our claim,
In every loss, we rise the same.

Each challenge met, a lesson learned,
In fiery paths, our spirits burned.
Together we stand, unbowed, unbent,
In the face of fear, our hearts are sent.

So let us march, with heads held high,
Through storms that rage and clouds that cry.
For in this bond, we find our strength,
The covenant drawn, in love's great length.

Embrace the dawn, renew the quest,
In courage's name, we find our rest.
With every step, our hopes ignite,
The covenant of courage brings forth light.

Sacred Ground of the Soul

In tranquil fields where silence grows,
We tread upon this holy prose.
With every step, a sacred prayer,
In grounded faith, we find our care.

The earth beneath, a tapestry,
Woven with love, a legacy.
In unity, we nurture dreams,
On sacred ground, hope softly gleams.

Through seasons change, our spirits rise,
In nature's arms, we claim the skies.
With hearts attuned to nature's song,
We find our place where we belong.

So let us gather, hand in hand,
Upon this soul, this cherished land.
For in each moment, we discover,
The sacred ground connects each other.

With gentle whispers, we shall share,
In sacred love, our voices pair.
Together we'll stand, unafraid, unbowed,
On sacred ground, we are avowed.

The Beacon of Authenticity

In a world of shadows cast,
I shine with truth, steadfast.
Guided by the light within,
A journey where I begin.

In every doubt, I stand tall,
Embracing love, I hear the call.
Authentic soul, pure and bright,
A beacon shining in the night.

With every step, I seek the way,
In honesty, I choose to stay.
The whispers of my heart, I lead,
In the quiet, my spirit freed.

Courage flows from knowing me,
A promise in humility.
In every moment, I find grace,
In my truth, I find my place.

Each challenge met with open hands,
In faith, my heart forever stands.
With strength, I rise, my spirit glows,
In authenticity, love bestows.

A Vessel for My True Nature

Crafted from the heavens' clay,
A vessel formed to find my way.
In quietude, I seek the core,
Of love and light forevermore.

Gently, I embrace my grace,
Reflecting truth, a sacred space.
Each heartbeat sings a holy song,
In unity, I feel I belong.

Transparent soul, I welcome all,
In every rise, I heed the call.
A vessel pure, I'm made to share,
Compassion flows; I breathe in prayer.

Through trials, I find my strength,
In every challenge, I go the length.
With love as my unwavering guide,
Within my heart, faith will abide.

With open arms, I hold the world,
In every moment, dreams unfurled.
A vessel filled with love, I sea,
To share the joy of being free.

Faithful Resilience

Through tempests fierce, I rise and stand,
With heart and soul, I clasp His hand.
A whisper soft within my core,
Encouragement that I adore.

In trials faced, my spirit sways,
Yet through the dark, my heart conveys.
With every fall, I learn to soar,
Resilience born forevermore.

With faith as shield, I brave the night,
In shadows deep, I find the light.
Each setback fuels my sacred fire,
In struggles met, I grow higher.

My burdens lifted, grace bestowed,
In faithful love, the path is showed.
Through brokenness, wholeness brings,
A symphony of endless rings.

In every heartbeat, strength I find,
With gentle whispers, love's aligned.
Resilient heart, a truth profound,
In faithful hope, my soul is crowned.

Steadfast in the Storm

Winds may howl, and skies may grey,
Yet in my soul, I find the way.
Rooted deep in sacred ground,
In faith and hope, I am unbound.

The storm may rage, but I will stand,
A heart held firm, a steady hand.
With courage drawn from love's embrace,
Each tempest faced, a sacred place.

In moments dark, I seek the spark,
Illuminating from afar.
With every wave, I'll rise again,
In steadfast love, there is no end.

Through trials fierce, I see the light,
A promise born from darkest night.
In unity, I stand as one,
With faith and hope, the battle's won.

In turbulent seas, I sail with grace,
Each storm embraced, a holy space.
Steadfast heart, my soul will soar,
In love's embrace, forevermore.

Anchored by Celestial Whispers

In stillness, I hear the celestial call,
A gentle murmur, guiding through it all.
Stars twinkle above, like dreams above,
In the heart, there's a whisper of love.

Each dawn brings light, a heavenly grace,
In shadows of doubt, I find my place.
Guided by faith, my spirit shall soar,
To realms of the sacred, forevermore.

Anchored in truth, my soul takes flight,
Through trials and tempests, I seek the light.
With every breath, I embrace the divine,
A journey of trust, in the celestial design.

Moments of silence, where grace flows free,
In silence, the secrets of eternity.
Each heartbeat, a promise, a sacred embrace,
In the whispers of night, I find my grace.

Forever anchored, in love's gentle tide,
Through struggles and storms, I shall abide.
Celestial whispers, a guide from above,
In the depths of my heart, I am filled with love.

The Altar of Self-Discovery

Upon the altar, I lay my fears,
A sacred space, where truth appears.
With every tear, a piece of me grows,
In the warmth of acceptance, my spirit glows.

The mirror reflects, what I wish to see,
In shadows and light, I discover me.
Each step on this path, a lesson unfolds,
In the depths of my soul, my story is told.

Surrendering doubt, I rise from the dust,
In the grace of the journey, I learn to trust.
With open hands, I embrace what is mine,
The altar of self, where my heart will shine.

Through struggles and questions, I seek the truth,
In the innocence lost, I find my youth.
With every heartbeat, I gather the light,
A journey of love, through day and night.

On the altar of self, I kneel and pray,
For wisdom and courage, to guide my way.
In acceptance and love, I find my decree,
The endless reflection, the essence of me.

Stars Within: The Celestial Reflection

Gaze into the soul, where starlight dwells,
A cosmos of dreams, where silence swells.
The universe whispers, secrets untold,
In the heart's quiet chambers, the stories unfold.

Each spark of light, a wish in the night,
Guiding my spirit, with celestial height.
In the tapestry woven, the stars align,
Reflecting the love, infinitely divine.

Journey inward, where mysteries bloom,
In the garden of faith, dispelling the gloom.
With each heartbeat, the rhythms entwine,
Revealing the strength, like stars, I shine.

In the quiet moments, I find my peace,
As stardust and spirit, together increase.
With grace as my compass, I navigate fate,
Embracing the cosmos, I am never late.

The stars within, a reminder I find,
In the vastness above, my essence is kind.
Through trials and triumphs, my spirit does soar,
In the deep of my being, I discover much more.

A Pilgrimage Through Inner Realms

In the sacred journey, I wander deep,
Through inner realms, where secrets sleep.
With every step, my heart takes flight,
In the stillness, I seek the light.

Mountains of doubt, I bravely face,
Each shadow a challenge, a sacred space.
Through valleys of sorrow, I carve my way,
With faith as my guide, I embrace each day.

The pilgrimage calls, as the spirit unfolds,
In the whispers of wisdom, the truth beholds.
With courage and love, I traverse the vast,
Embracing each moment, my soul is unmasked.

Amongst ancient echoes, I find my voice,
In the heart of the silence, I hear my choice.
With every heartbeat, the journey's embrace,
In the realms of the spirit, I find my place.

A pilgrimage vast, with wonders to seek,
In the voyage within, my heart learns to speak.
Through trials and triumphs, I rise from my dawn,
In the dance of the spirit, I am reborn.

The Echoes of My Inner Voice

In silence deep, my spirit speaks,
Whispers of truth, the heart still seeks.
Guiding me through the shadowed night,
A beacon glows, a flickering light.

Each word a promise, each breath a prayer,
In the stillness, I find my care.
With every echo, my doubts all cease,
The voice within, it grants me peace.

When the storms of life begin to rage,
My inner voice turns another page.
A song of courage in trials faced,
In sacred rhythms, my fears replaced.

The world may crumble, but I stand tall,
For in My heart, I hear Love's call.
Through valleys low, and mountains high,
My inner voice, my wings to fly.

As I walk the path, hand in hand,
With faith as my guide, in this holy land.
The echoes tell of journeys past,
In the heart's rhythm, my truths are cast.

The Covenant of Resilient Spirit

In the arms of grace, I make my stand,
A covenant written, in sacred sand.
With every challenge, I learn to rise,
The strength within, a gift from the skies.

My spirit resilient, unwavering fire,
Fulfilling the promise of a soul's desire.
Through trials and tears, I come to see,
The beauty of faith that sets me free.

Each storm that rages, a lesson learned,
In the furnace of struggle, my heart has burned.
Through shadows deep, my vision clears,
Crafting courage from my deepest fears.

With every breath, I seal this vow,
A testament written in the here and now.
For I am anchored, through joy and strife,
In the covenant of this sacred life.

Together we rise, as one we stand,
In the dance of divinity, hand in hand.
As the sun breaks through, in vibrant light,
My spirit's journey, forever bright.

Emblems of Inner Strength

In the tapestry of life, I weave my thread,
Each emblem of strength, by grace I'm led.
With faith as my armor, and love as my sword,
I stand unyielding, a truth restored.

Through the winds of change, my heart stays true,
In every struggle, my spirit renews.
With pillars of hope, I forge my way,
Guided by light, turning night into day.

The scars I carry, are badges of pride,
For in every fall, I find the guide.
Resilience blooms in gardens of pain,
Transforming the hurt into vibrant gain.

With every heartbeat, courage ignites,
Emblems of strength shine in darkest nights.
The roots run deep, and the branches soar,
Binding me to life, forevermore.

In the eye of the storm, my spirit will rise,
Grounded in truth, beneath vast skies.
I am unbreakable, I stand and I sing,
In the vessel of faith, my spirit takes wing.

The Halo of My Soul's Journey

In the glow of dawn, my spirit takes flight,
A halo of light that sparkles bright.
Across the horizon, where dreams entwine,
The essence of love in every sign.

Each step I take, a sacred dance,
With the universe whispering its romance.
Through valleys of sorrow, rivers of grace,
I find my way to a timeless place.

The halo that shines, a mirror of soul,
Reflecting the truth, making me whole.
Through shadows of doubt, it gently glows,
Guiding my heart where love freely flows.

In the tapestry woven, threads intertwine,
Stories of ages, a legacy divine.
With every heartbeat, I learn and grow,
A journey eternal, a vibrant flow.

As I walk this path, hand in hand with fate,
The halo of wisdom opens the gate.
With gratitude deep, and faith as my song,
I journey onward, where I belong.

The Sacred Roots of My Being

In the stillness, whispers call,
Seeded deep within my soul.
A sacred light begins to bloom,
Binding me to the divine whole.

Each moment grown in sacred soil,
Nurtured by prayer and grace.
In trials deep, I find my strength,
I stand firm in this holy place.

Raindrops fall like gentle tears,
Watering dreams of love and peace.
From ancient roots, my spirit rises,
In faith, my burdens find release.

With branches wide, I reach for skies,
Embracing both the sun and shade.
In harmony, my heart expands,
In nature's arms, I am remade.

The sacred roots entwine my path,
Their whispers guide my humble way.
In every leaf, a lesson learned,
In every breath, the gift of day.

When the Heart Knows Its Way

At dawn's first light, the heart awakes,
With whispers soft, it starts to sway.
Each pulse a truth, each beat a prayer,
Guiding me gently, come what may.

Through valleys deep and mountains high,
I walk the path where dreams abide.
With faith to light each step I take,
My heart's true compass, my undying guide.

In every smile, in every touch,
I feel the love that flows through me.
A river deep, a boundless sea,
Unity found, in all that's free.

When shadows fall and doubts arise,
I turn within, to find my calm.
The heart knows well, it speaks to me,
In sacred stillness, I find my balm.

Each moment cherished, no fear remains,
As love unfolds in skies so gray.
In the quiet glow of my own truth,
I walk the road where the heart knows its way.

The Mirror of My Faith

In the quiet night, a light does shine,
A mirror reflecting the soul's true face.
In every doubt, in every hope,
I seek the truth of love's embrace.

With every struggle, a lesson learned,
In shadows cast, I find my way.
The mirror holds my deepest fears,
But through the glass, I see the day.

Each tear I shed, a drop of light,
Reflecting strength and grace within.
The mirror shows my sacred worth,
In every loss, there blooms a win.

In faith's embrace, I find my peace,
Through trials faced, I rise anew.
The mirror of my faith reveals,
The radiant love that guides me through.

With open heart, I learn to see,
In every challenge, blessings flow.
The mirror carries me on high,
In faith, forever, love's light glows.

Woven in the Fabric of Belief

Each thread a story, richly spun,
Woven tightly, love's soft embrace.
In every stitch, a whispered prayer,
Binding hearts in sacred space.

The fabric holds our hopes and dreams,
A tapestry of light and grace.
In unity, our spirits soar,
Together we find our rightful place.

With colors bright, we paint our paths,
Through darker days, we hold the line.
In every heart, a spark ignites,
Woven by love, forever divine.

Through storms that rage, through trials long,
We stand as one, unbreakable thread.
In harmony, our voices rise,
A symphony of faith well-spread.

As life unfolds in sacred ways,
We cherish each new dawn and leaf.
In the vast quilt of the universe,
We find our joy, woven in belief.

The Blessed Assurance of Being

In the stillness, I find my grace,
A gentle whisper, a sacred space.
Each breath a gift, each moment divine,
In the light of faith, my spirit shall shine.

Through shadows deep, I walk with trust,
In the hands of love, I find my must.
With every trial, my heart grows strong,
In the heart of peace, I truly belong.

Hope blooms eternal in the soul's embrace,
Guided by light, I seek His face.
Provision abounds, my fears fade away,
In the warmth of His arms, I long to stay.

As rivers flow to the ocean wide,
My heart, it swells with a holy tide.
Each step I take, I feel His call,
In the love that binds, I shall never fall.

With faith as my anchor, I rise each day,
In the path of love, I find my way.
The blessed assurance, my heart's refrain,
In the peace of His grace, I'll ever remain.

A Soul's Serene Journey

Beyond the valleys, a whisper flows,
In every heart, a purpose grows.
The journey unfolds, serene and clear,
Guided by faith, I have nothing to fear.

Mountains may rise, yet I shall tread,
In quiet assurance, I forge ahead.
Each step a prayer, each pause a sigh,
In the dance of life, I learn to fly.

With each sunrise, His mercy I see,
The grace that envelops and sets me free.
Through trials faced and lessons learned,
In the light of His love, forever I'm turned.

The stars above sing of beauty rare,
In the silence of night, my soul lays bare.
A tapestry woven with threads of light,
With faith as my guide, I embrace the night.

In the quiet moments, I hear the call,
A symphony of love that stirs my all.
With every heartbeat, my spirit soars,
In the arms of grace, my soul explores.

The Disciple of Inner Peace

In the garden of stillness, I sow my seeds,
With tender whispers, the spirit leads.
Roots dug deep in the soil of light,
Flourishing grace, banishing fright.

Beneath the stars, I find my place,
A tranquil heart, a holy grace.
With every breath, I witness the flow,
In the river of calm, my spirit shall grow.

Through turmoil's storm, I hold my ground,
In the eye of the tempest, peace can be found.
Lessons learned in the trials of night,
In the depth of silence, I embrace the light.

Each thought a prayer, each moment a chance,
To dance with the divine in sacred romance.
As whispers of love cradle my soul,
In the depths of peace, I am whole.

A disciple of stillness, a seeker of grace,
In the breath of life, I find my place.
With joy in the journey, I tread this way,
In the harmony of being, I forever stay.

Faith's Embrace

In the warmth of faith, I find my rest,
With open arms, I am truly blessed.
Each dawn a promise, each dusk a prayer,
In the heart of the sacred, I'm always aware.

Through trials faced, I learn to trust,
In the depths of worry, I rise from dust.
Every moment of doubt, I courageously face,
In the glow of belief, I find my place.

With every heartbeat, hope runs deep,
In silence and solitude, I shall keep.
The gentle whispers of love surround,
In the embrace of faith, true peace is found.

As rivers merge into the sea,
My spirit longs to be truly free.
In the fabric of love, I'm woven tight,
In faith's embrace, I bask in the light.

Stepping boldly into the unknown,
In the arms of grace, I've surely grown.
With faith as my guide, forever I roam,
In the depths of the heart, I have found my home.

Tides of Tranquility

In silence flows the gentle stream,
Where hope blooms bright and faith redeems.
The stars above in stillness glow,
Guiding souls on paths they go.

Each wave a whisper, soft and pure,
Embracing hearts with love's allure.
The moon, a beacon, lights the night,
Awakening dreams with silver light.

In nature's arms, we find our peace,
A moment's grace, our souls release.
With every breath, we feel His grace,
In tranquil tides, we find our place.

The world may storm, yet we stand firm,
With prayer our shelter, faith our balm.
In unity, our spirits rise,
Together drawn to heaven's skies.

Tides may ebb, and tides may flow,
Yet in His love, we always know.
In tranquil waters, fears subside,
In sacred trust, our hearts abide.

The Covenant of Perseverance

In trials faced, our spirits soar,
With steadfast hearts, we seek and more.
The promise made, we shall not break,
With every step, His path we take.

When shadows linger, hope will gleam,
A guiding star, a radiant dream.
With courage drawn from living word,
In sacred strength, our voices stirred.

Through storms of doubt, we rise anew,
Our faith, a shield, our aim so true.
In unity, we stand as one,
Beneath the gaze of moon and sun.

From every tear, a lesson learned,
In every heart, His light discerned.
With courage firm, we march ahead,
In covenant strong, through love we're led.

For every trial that we face,
A promise keeps us, full of grace.
With faith unshaken, we endure,
In Him, our souls forever secure.

In the Presence of the Most High

In the quiet hush of evening's breath,
We gather close, we seek the depths.
In reverent awe, our spirits rise,
In the presence of the Most High.

With open hearts, we humbly kneel,
In whispered prayers, His love we feel.
In every moment, grace abounds,
In sacred stillness, peace surrounds.

The light that shines within our core,
A flame ignited, forevermore.
Through valleys low, through mountains high,
We walk with hope, we trust, we cry.

In trials faced, He walks beside,
With every tear, our fears subside.
His gentle voice, a guiding light,
Our hearts ignite in love's pure plight.

In communion sweet, our souls unite,
In jubilant songs that take to flight.
With every breath, His name we sing,
In the presence of the Most High, we cling.

As dusk gives way to morning's glow,
We rise renewed, our spirits flow.
In faith and love, we find our way,
In the Most High's arms, forever stay.

Fortress of Solitude

In quiet corners, where shadows play,
We find our refuge, night and day.
A fortress built on love and care,
In solitude, His whispers bear.

The world outside may roar and shout,
Yet in this stillness, we find out.
Each thought a prayer, each breath a hymn,
In sanctuary's arms, we grow within.

With every heartbeat, peace is found,
In sacred spaces, grace abounds.
Here burdens lifted, wounds are healed,
In solitude, our souls revealed.

The shadows dance, the light enfolds,
In quiet strength, we break the molds.
With every sigh, we rise above,
In fortress strong, we're wrapped in love.

Through trials faced, we stand our ground,
A mighty wall where hope is found.
In solitude, our hearts align,
In His embrace, our souls entwine.

As storms may lash and tempest roar,
Within these walls, we are restored.
In fortress of solitude, we trust,
In faith's embrace, we rise from dust.

Drawn by Grace

In shadows deep, I search for light,
A whispered prayer, a guiding sight.
Through valleys low, my spirit soars,
For in His arms, my heart restores.

With every step, I tread with faith,
In trials faced, I find my place.
His boundless love, a gentle breeze,
Awakens hope, my soul at ease.

Though burdens lend their heavy weight,
I trust in Him to guide my fate.
The path may twist, the night may fall,
Yet grace will be my steadfast call.

In service true, I seek His will,
With open hands, my heart stands still.
Through acts of love, His light I share,
To lift the world with tender care.

A vessel pure, for mercy's flow,
In every heart, His seed I sow.
Drawn by His grace, I rise anew,
In endless joy, my spirit true.

The Fortress of Resolve

Within my heart, a fortress stands,
Built of faith and gentle hands.
Against the storms, it holds the ground,
In quiet strength, my hope is found.

When shadows creep and fears arise,
I lift my gaze to endless skies.
A voice within, so firm and clear,
Reminds me that my God is near.

With every trial, a lesson learned,
In every flame, the spirit burned.
Resilience flows like rivers wide,
In God's embrace, I will abide.

The walls may tremble, but I stand strong,
In harmony, I find my song.
Unyielding heart, I seek to serve,
With grace and love, my soul preserve.

Together forged in light divine,
In unity, our spirits shine.
The fortress built, a sacred pact,
With every breath, I shall act.

In trials passed, we rise above,
Empowered by His endless love.
The fortress stands, forever true,
In Him, I find my strength anew.

Unbroken by Doubt

When shadows whisper in the night,
And doubts arise, I seek the light.
A steady heart, with faith ablaze,
I walk the path of His sweet grace.

Each fear a cloud that drifts away,
In trust, I find my hope today.
Through trials fierce, I stand my ground,
In every pain, His love is found.

The storms may roar, but I am still,
His gentle voice inspires my will.
An anchor firm, my soul embraced,
Unbroken by doubt, I run the race.

Each doubt, a pebble on my way,
I cast aside, choose light today.
In solid rock, I build my stand,
With courage raised, I clasp His hand.

Unseen but felt, the spirit's guide,
With every step, in Him I bide.
A heart of hope, I freely shout,
In faith alone, I'm unbroken by doubt.

Songs of the Soul's Strength

A melody born from depths within,
In trials faced, I rise again.
The songs of faith, they fill the air,
An anthem strong, a heartfelt prayer.

With every breath, I lift my voice,
In rhythms sweet, I make my choice.
To sing of love, to share the light,
In shadows cast, I find my sight.

The chorus swells, as hearts unite,
In harmony divine and bright.
With souls ablaze, we stand as one,
In songs of strength, our hearts are spun.

Though storms may rage and winds may blow,
In every note, His kindness flows.
Thus, I will feel the spirit's lift,
With each refrain, a sacred gift.

This song of life, I shall proclaim,
In every heart, ignite the flame.
For in our strength, His love we find,
In songs of the soul, forever bind.

Faith's Whisper in the Silence

In stillness deep, the spirit speaks,
A gentle call, where quiet seeks.
The heart, it listens with bated breath,
A promise lies beyond the death.

Through shadows dark, the light will grow,
A guiding star in night's soft glow.
With every prayer, a bond is sewn,
In whispered grace, the truth is known.

When doubts arise, and fears conspire,
The flame of hope will never tire.
With open hands, I let love flow,
In faith, I trust, in peace, I'll go.

Each tear, a seed of strength and grace,
In trials faced, I find my place.
The silence hums with sacred song,
In faith's embrace, I will belong.

Beneath the veil of night's embrace,
I find the light, a warm solace.
In every heartbeat, love's refrain,
A whispered truth that will sustain.

The Shield of My Existence

When storms arise and shadows stir,
With faith, my heart begins to blur.
In sacred trust, I find my might,
The shield of love dispels the night.

Each prayer I send, a hand of grace,
In trials faced, I find my place.
With courage firm, I stand and fight,
The light of truth will spark the bright.

A fortress built on hope and dream,
In unity, we find the stream.
Together strong, we face the gale,
In love's embrace, we will prevail.

With every breath, a vow I keep,
In rhythms deep, my spirit leaps.
The shield, a bond that will not break,
In sacred trust, I claim my stake.

So through the fire and through the dark,
I'll carry forth my sacred spark.
With faith as guard, I'll brave the storm,
In love's embrace, forever warm.

Beneath the Canopy of Belief

In twilight's glow, beneath the trees,
My heart is stilled by gentle breeze.
Each leaf, a testament of grace,
In nature's arms, I find my place.

Above me spreads the sky so wide,
In faith, I seek a loving guide.
The stars, they whisper ancient tales,
Of journeys past and strength that prevails.

With every step on this sacred ground,
In silence deep, my hopes abound.
Amidst the shadows, light will seep,
Beneath this canopy, I will keep.

Each moment shared, a gift divine,
In gratitude, my spirit shines.
With open heart and open mind,
In every soul, a love I find.

So let me walk with gentle grace,
In every glance, a warm embrace.
Beneath the canopy of belief,
I find in love my sweet relief.

Sanctum of Unwavering Courage

In quiet halls, the heart's resolve,
In sacred space, our fears dissolve.
With steadfast faith, we rise anew,
In courage found, our spirits grew.

Through trials fierce and daunting maze,
We stand as one, in hope we gaze.
Each challenge faced, a lesson learned,
In fires forged, our passions burned.

With hands held high and voices strong,
United here, we all belong.
In every heart, a battle cried,
In faith's embrace, we will abide.

When darkness looms, and doubts creep near,
We'll light the way, dispel the fear.
With courage bold, we speak the truth,
In love's embrace, we find our youth.

So let us walk this path of grace,
In every moment, we find our place.
The sanctum of our steadfast heart,
In love's sweet dance, we play our part.

From Barren Soil to Abundant Grace

In barren soil where hope lay still,
Seeds of faith, with gentle will,
God's hands nurture, bless the ground,
From ashes rise, new life is found.

Through trials dark, the path unfolds,
A journey worth, in grace we're told,
With tender roots, we reach the sky,
In heavy burdens, spirits fly.

The sun shall shine on hearts anew,
In every shade, His love breaks through,
From desolation, blooms arise,
A testament that never dies.

With waters pure, we quench our thirst,
In gratitude, our souls are versed,
For grace bestowed upon our days,
We sing in joy, our hearts ablaze.

We harvest joy from sacrifice,
In fields of mercy, hearts entice,
For every struggle, every tear,
In God's embrace, we cast out fear.

The Testament of Inner Light

Within the soul, a spark so bright,
A flame of truth, our guiding light,
In darkest nights, it shines and warms,
Through tempests fierce, it keeps us calm.

Each breath we take, a prayer we weave,
In silent moments, we believe,
With humble hearts, we seek His face,
In every trial, we find His grace.

The world may dim, its voices loud,
But in our hearts, we stand unbowed,
For love divine, it shelters deep,
In quiet faith, our spirits leap.

Reflections dance in sacred space,
A testament to His embrace,
With gratitude, our song we raise,
To honor Him, we sing His praise.

In every soul, His light does dwell,
A heavenly truth, a holy shell,
So let us shine, be brave and true,
For in His love, we are made new.

Crowned with Resilience

With heavy crowns of thorny care,
We find our strength in fervent prayer,
Through trials faced, our spirits grow,
In darkest hours, His light will show.

Resilience breeds in hearts of clay,
With every fall, we rise, we sway,
For in the struggle, lessons learned,
Through tears of grief, our hearts have burned.

A crown of thorns transforms to gold,
In every story, courage bold,
With steadfast faith, we shall endure,
For love's embrace, our hearts are pure.

In soaring heights or valleys low,
Through winds of change, we learn to grow,
With every beat, we echo grace,
A testament to faith's embrace.

So let us stand, our heads held high,
Crowned with resilience, we defy,
For in each trial, we find the key,
To living life in harmony.

The Soul's Song of Survival

In whispered winds, the soul will sing,
Of trials faced, and what they bring,
A melody of strength and grace,
The song of life we must embrace.

Through storms we march, our spirits bold,
With every story, truth unfolds,
For in adversity, we find our worth,
The sacred dance of life, our birth.

Though shadows loom and doubts arise,
We lift our hearts, we claim the skies,
For in our souls, a fire ignites,
To face the dawn, to claim our rights.

With every heartbeat, every sigh,
A testament that will not die,
For steel is forged through fire's test,
Our souls rejoice in every quest.

The echoes of survival ring,
In harmony, our voices cling,
For in this life we stand as one,
A symphony of love begun.

The Promise of Personal Faith

In whispers soft, the heart believes,
A sacred bond, the soul receives.
Each prayer a seed, in silence sown,
In every trial, faith has grown.

Through darkest nights, the spirit shines,
With every step, the path aligns.
A light of hope, through doubts' embrace,
In trust, we find our sacred space.

In storms that rage, we find our calm,
With trust in Him, our hearts are balm.
A promise kept, a guiding star,
In faith's embrace, we've come so far.

Together we walk, on holy ground,
Where love and grace, forever abound.
Each moment counts, in His great plan,
For in His arms, all are one, we stand.

With every breath, we seek His face,
In every heart, a thread of grace.
The promise made, through trials faced,
In personal faith, we find our place.

The Strength Found in Shadows

In shadows deep, where whispers dwell,
Strength rises up, a sacred well.
In quiet moments, fear takes flight,
For in the dark, we find the light.

When burdens weigh, and spirits tire,
In faith's embrace, we rise higher.
The trials faced, a path to grow,
Through hidden depths, the heart can glow.

Each shadow cast, a lesson taught,
In silence deep, our battles fought.
Revealing strength, we never knew,
In divine hands, all things renew.

Though storms may rage, and winds may howl,
In shadows' fold, we hear the howl.
For in the depths, a flicker gleams,
The strength we find, fuels our dreams.

So let us tread, through trials wide,
In every shadow, faith our guide.
For strength unveiled, in darkness found,
In God's embrace, we stand unbound.

Radiance of Inner Faith

A gentle spark, ignites the soul,
Within the heart, the light takes toll.
In every thought, a prayer unfolds,
The radiance of faith, bright and bold.

In daily walks, through life's embrace,
We feel His love, a warm grace.
Through trials faced, we learn to trust,
In God alone, we place our thrust.

Each challenge met, a chance to grow,
With inner faith, we boldly show.
That strength resides in our true heart,
In every moment, He is our part.

From inner depths, the courage springs,
In faith we find, the joy it brings.
A luminous glow, from deep within,
In every loss, there's always win.

So shine, dear heart, let light abound,
In faith's embrace, forever found.
The radiance of joy, pure and bright,
In every step, we walk in light.

The Quiet Confidence

In stillness found, a voice so clear,
Whispers calm the doubts and fear.
The quiet strength, within the core,
In gentle grace, we find much more.

With every breath, a promise true,
In faith's embrace, we are renewed.
An inner peace, though storms may rage,
In trust we turn, another page.

The quiet confidence that shines,
In every heart, the spirit twines.
For when we trust, the way unfolds,
A life transformed, with stories told.

In moments sweet, where silence reigns,
We hear His whispers, break the chains.
The calm resolve, a steady mind,
In gentle faith, our hearts aligned.

So walk in trust, and let it be,
The quiet confidence, setting free.
For in that space, we find our grace,
A sacred journey, a holy place.

The Anchor of My Inner Peace

In stillness I find grace,
A whisper in the quiet place.
Heaven's light upon my soul,
Resting in the timeless whole.

Each storm shall pass, each trial cease,
With faith, my heart shall find release.
The tide may rise, but I will stand,
For Love, as anchoring hand.

In prayer, my spirit finds its song,
A melody both pure and strong.
In every breath, a sacred chance,
To trust in the eternal dance.

With every dawn, a promise new,
In shadows cast, the light breaks through.
A tranquil heart, a steady grace,
Guides me to my heart's true place.

The Spiral of Self-Affirmation

In every step, I find my way,
A journey bright as dawn's first ray.
With each truth, my spirit grows,
A sacred trust that always flows.

I rise anew in every fall,
A voice within that calls us all.
In humble words, my spirit sings,
Awakening the faith it brings.

The mirror shows my shining grace,
A glimpse of Him in every face.
Beloved, I embrace my worth,
A child of light, forever birthed.

In circles wide, I chant my song,
Together we are brave and strong.
With every heartbeat, every breath,
I celebrate this life, not death.

The Pilgrim's Heartbeat

In solitude, my heart responds,
To whispered love, through endlessponds.
Each footstep marks a sacred quest,
With faith my journey feels like rest.

From mountain high to valley low,
The pilgrim's path is where I'll go.
With every trial, my spirit grows,
In every heart, the spirit flows.

A bond of brotherhood I find,
In laughter shared, our joys entwined.
Each stranger met has much to share,
In stories wrapped in silent prayer.

Through winding roads and endless skies,
I seek the truth where wisdom lies.
A heartbeat quickens, a flame ignites,
On this path of sacred sights.

Beneath the Veil of Divine Love

In quiet moments, grace unfolds,
A tapestry of tales retold.
Beneath the veil of love divine,
My heart aligns, your heart as mine.

Soft whispers cradle weary souls,
In wounded hearts, a new life rolls.
With arms outstretched, I find my home,
In every heart, no one alone.

The light of love will never fade,
In every choice, my fears betrayed.
Together we rise, together we soar,
In unity, forevermore.

Through trials faced, a bond is spun,
Each tear, a seed of faith begun.
Beneath your veil, I softly see,
The divine love that sets me free.

A Sojourn in Self-Reflection

In silence I wander, deep thoughts arise,
A mirror of spirit, in truth it replies.
Each moment a lesson, each breath a prayer,
Guided by whispers, divine and rare.

The shadows within me, they gently unfold,
Secrets of wisdom, waiting to be told.
With faith as my anchor, I embrace the night,
In darkness I ponder, I search for the light.

A journey within, to find what is real,
The heart has a rhythm that time cannot steal.
With courage I step through the veil of my mind,
Unraveling layers, my essence defined.

Each thought a reflection on waters so clear,
The soul's quiet yearning, a song I can hear.
In the stillness, I blossom, the past holds no sting,
Rejoicing in presence, I'm learning to sing.

This sojourn of truth, a sacred embrace,
As I walk with humility, I find my place.
In the depths of my being, the spirit ignites,
Illuminating paths with celestial lights.

In the Embrace of My Essence

In the stillness I gather, my essence calls,
Wrapped in the softness, where love never falls.
Each heartbeat a message, a hymn from above,
Caressing the shadows with radiant love.

I stand on the brink of a boundless sea,
Waves of compassion, they carry me free.
In the embrace of my spirit, I find my way,
Guided by whispers that never betray.

Through valleys of longing, the heart's gentle song,
Reminds me of grace, where I truly belong.
With each step I take, I walk hand in hand,
With the light of my essence, forever I stand.

The world is a canvas, painted in dreams,
By visions of faith that flow in soft streams.
In the depths of my being, I reach for the sky,
And dance with the stars as they silently fly.

In love's vast expanse, I discover my truth,
The whispers of ages, the wisdom of youth.
In the embrace of my essence, I find my grace,
An eternal reflection, a sacred space.

The Quiet Power Within

In the hush of the dawn, where the stillness breathes,
A power awakens, the spirit achieves.
Soft echoes of strength flow deep in my core,
A flame that ignites, forever to soar.

With patience I gather the gifts of the soul,
In the silence I listen, to make myself whole.
A river of wisdom, so deep and profound,
In the quiet I flourish, my essence unbound.

Each heartbeat a prayer, each thought a decree,
In the calm I discover what's true, what's to be.
The power of stillness, a treasure to find,
As I journey within, with a peaceful mind.

Through valleys of doubt and shadows of fear,
The quiet power whispers, forever near.
In the echoes of silence, my spirit takes flight,
A beacon of love in the depths of the night.

So here I stand firmly, in strength I believe,
A testament to all who dare to perceive.
In the quiet, my power, a truth yet untold,
Awakens the fire, a destiny bold.

Chosen by the Light of Truth

In the glow of the dawn, where shadows retreat,
I walk on this journey, my purpose complete.
Chosen by light that illuminates ways,
A pathway of promise in each blessed gaze.

The truth is a beacon, so vivid, so clear,
A compass of love, instilled without fear.
In the depths of my heart, a song whispers bright,
Guiding my steps through the dark of the night.

Each moment a mirror, reflecting the grace,
Of choosing the light, in this sacred space.
I shed the illusions that once held me tight,
Embracing the wisdom, the power of light.

With each passing day, my spirit ascends,
In unity found, the journey transcends.
A tapestry woven with threads of pure love,
Reminding me gently of blessings above.

Chosen by truth, I rise ever higher,
A vessel of hope, my soul's true desire.
In the warmth of the light, I find my rebirth,
As I walk in the presence of limitless worth.

Gleaning Light from Shadows

In the depths of night I seek,
A whisper in the silence speaks,
Guiding me towards the dawn,
Where faith and hope are never gone.

From shadows cast, I rise anew,
With every step, I find the true,
The light that shines within my soul,
A comforting warmth that makes me whole.

Through trials faced, I learn to see,
The lessons hidden gracefully,
In darkness, light begins to grow,
Compassion blooms and love will flow.

Lifted by the gentle breeze,
I feel the beckoning of trees,
Their branches bowing in repose,
A sacred dance, the Spirit flows.

With every heartbeat, dreams ignite,
As shadows dance with morning light,
In unity, all hearts we bind,
The sacred truth we seek to find.

The Call of My Inner Prayer

Oh, sacred silence, hear my plea,
In whispers soft, I come to thee,
A yearning heart, a restless soul,
In prayer, I find my being whole.

The echoes of my spirit soar,
In every moment, I implore,
With faith as my unwavering guide,
I open wide my heart to bide.

The trust I place in unseen grace,
A gentle touch, a warm embrace,
In stillness, wisdom starts to flow,
And in that space, my spirit knows.

In every prayer, I find my way,
A melody that will not sway,
It lifts my soul, it lights my path,
With every word, I feel God's wrath.

When shadows gather, bold and near,
I breathe and let go of my fear,
For in the quiet, I discern,
The sacred flame, a soul's return.

Fostering Flames of Trust

Within the hearth of faith I stand,
A flicker bright in time's vast hand,
Each flame a promise, each light a vow,
In trust, I rise, in trust, I bow.

The embers dance beneath the night,
A testament to hope's own light,
In every trial, a spark defines,
The strength within these heart-felt lines.

Together we gather, hearts ablaze,
With love and truth that never sways,
Through storms we walk, in union strong,
In woven fates, we find our song.

Come, hold my hand as we embrace,
The warmth of faith, a sacred space,
In sharing burdens, joy shall grow,
A flame sustained, together flow.

As trust ignites, we pave the way,
For brighter tomorrows, come what may,
In every flicker, God does call,
Together we rise, together we fall.

The Communion of Spirit and Self

In solitude, my spirit rests,
A sacred bond that never quests,
In quiet moments, truth reveals,
The whispers soft, a grace that heals.

Amidst the noise of worldly strife,
I seek the pulse of sacred life,
In breath, the universe aligns,
A fusion sweet, our path enshrines.

Through every doubt, I find my way,
In communion's grace, I choose to stay,
The heart's deep longing, soul's embrace,
In unity, we find our place.

Alone together, we ascend,
In sacred circles, hearts we mend,
With open arms, I welcome all,
In love's embrace, we rise, not fall.

For in the depth of who we are,
Our spirits dance, a shining star,
Together woven, whole and blessed,
In communion's light, our souls find rest.

The Solace of Sanctity

In the quiet of prayer, hearts align,
Seeking solace, a love divine.
Whispers of grace in sacred night,
Embracing the path, the holy light.

In the stillness, we find our way,
Every moment, a chance to stay.
Faith like a river, flows pure and free,
Carving the soul, a path to see.

With humble offerings, we come near,
Casting away the weight of fear.
In every breath, the Spirit speaks,
In love's embrace, our solace peaks.

Hearts open wide, with arms to share,
Finding comfort in the solemn air.
In unity's song, we rise anew,
Together in faith, eternally true.

The solace we search, within us lies,
In the sacred hearts, our spirit flies.
Together we stand, forever strong,
In the calm of sanctity, we belong.

The Gospel of Self-Reliance

In shadows cast, we seek the dawn,
A guiding star, our fears withdrawn.
With courage found, we rise and shine,
In faith's embrace, our hearts align.

The strength within us is divinely led,
In every trial, our spirits fed.
With each step taken, we forge our fate,
In self-reliance, we cultivate.

Through every storm, we stand as one,
With love's embrace, the battle won.
We learn to trust in our own grace,
In the gospel of life, we find our place.

The journey long, yet deeply sweet,
With every lesson, the heart's heartbeat.
Through valleys low, and peaks so high,
In self-reliance, we touch the sky.

In knowing self, we are made whole,
In the choir of life, we play our role.
With arms outstretched, we share our light,
In the gospel of strength, we take flight.

Beyond the fear, beyond the strife,
In self-reliance, we find true life.
In every breath, a promise true,
In the gospel's embrace, we renew.

Pilgrimage of the Heart

Upon the path, we journey slow,
With every step, our spirits grow.
In sacred places, we choose to tread,
In the pilgrimage, where faith is fed.

The heart alive, in sacred song,
In every beat, where we belong.
With prayers whispered into the night,
Our souls connect, with pure delight.

Through valleys deep and hills so high,
In seeking truth, we dare to fly.
With grace as guide, we walk with care,
In the pilgrimage, we seek to share.

With every lesson, the heart is stirred,
In moments gentle, our vision blurred.
Yet through the fog, the light will shine,
In pilgrimage, our hearts combine.

Together we rise, as one we stand,
In love's embrace, a promised land.
In every journey, we find our part,
In the pilgrimage, the way is art.

Through depths of faith, we chart the course,
With open hearts, we draw on force.
In every step, our spirits soar,
In the pilgrimage of the heart, we explore.

Enduring Light of the Spirit

In darkness deep, a light shall glow,
Guiding the lost, where hope can flow.
Through trials faced, we stand as one,
In enduring light, our race is run.

Each day we rise, with faith in hand,
Building bridges, where we can stand.
In love's embrace, our spirits sing,
In the enduring light, we find our wings.

In moments fraught with doubt and fear,
The spirit's whisper, ever near.
Through currents strong, we navigate,
In the light's warmth, we celebrate.

Together bound, we lift our gaze,
In the spirit's glow, we sing our praise.
With every heartbeat, the light persists,
In enduring love, the heart exists.

Through all the storms, the spirit's song,
In every struggle, we grow strong.
In unity's grace, we find our fight,
In the enduring light, we shine bright.

As shadows fade, we stand in grace,
In the light of spirit, we find our place.
Together we rise, forever free,
In the enduring light, we are meant to be.

The Strength of My Spirit's Song

In the silence, I find grace,
Harmony whispers in each place.
With faith, my heart takes flight,
A melody born of sacred light.

Every trial, a note embraced,
Resilience found in love's soft taste.
I sing for joy, I sing for peace,
In each refrain, my worries cease.

The echo of hope resounds within,
Guiding me through where I've been.
With each breath, I raise my voice,
In the stillness, I rejoice.

In shadows deep, I'll trust the song,
For through the dark, I will belong.
My spirit dances, bold and free,
In the music, I find Thee.

Let this hymn of love declare,
That in my heart, You always care.
For every note, a prayer ascends,
In harmony, my soul transcends.

Walking the Path of Inner Light

Upon the trail where shadows wane,
I seek the truth beyond the pain.
With each step, my spirit glows,
Guided by grace, the love that flows.

The lantern bright within me shines,
Illuminates the sacred signs.
I walk with faith, my heart in tow,
Each moment blooms, a chance to grow.

In silence, whispers softly call,
Reminding me I'm one with all.
The stars above, a guiding choir,
Each twinkle burns with holy fire.

Through valleys deep and mountains high,
My soul takes flight beneath the sky.
For in this journey, love is found,
In every pulse, in every sound.

With every tread, I feel Your grace,
In every breath, Your warm embrace.
As dawn unfolds the sacred light,
I walk the path, my spirit bright.

The Revelation of Quiet Resolve

In the stillness, strength is born,
A gentle spirit, like the dawn.
With hearts aligned, we stand as one,
Together, facing battles won.

The storm may rage, the winds may howl,
Yet in my heart, I hear Your vow.
With courage found in sacred space,
I find my path, a holy grace.

In whispers soft, I hear the call,
A love that conquers, brings the fall.
Through trials faced, I stand my ground,
In quiet resolve, my truth is found.

The light within, a steady flame,
Through darkest nights, I know Your name.
With every breath, I draw so near,
Faith blooms and calms my every fear.

In each heartbeat, resilience flows,
An inner strength that ever grows.
With every step, I choose to rise,
In love's embrace, my spirit flies.

In the Garden of My Heart

In the garden where blessings bloom,
Each petal holds a sacred room.
With gentle hands, I tend with care,
In every breath, Your love I share.

The seeds of faith, I plant with hope,
In the rich soil, my spirit will cope.
Through rain and sun, I nurture well,
In this garden, my soul will dwell.

The fragrance sweet of mercy's rose,
In paths of light, my spirit grows.
With each sunrise, a chance to start,
In the garden of my heart.

With every bloom, I find my way,
Through joy and sorrow, night and day.
In love's embrace, I find my rest,
In the garden, I am blessed.

So let me walk with faith anew,
In every moment, I seek You.
In joy and peace, I play my part,
In the garden of my heart.

Blossoms of the Spirit

In gardens where the virtues grow,
Each petal bathed in radiant glow.
The seeds of faith through trials sown,
In heart's embrace, the love is known.

From whispers soft, the spirits rise,
Transforming pain into the skies.
With every bloom, new life appears,
Uniting hope throughout the years.

Amidst the thorns, the grace unfolds,
A tapestry of stories told.
In every scent, a prayer is sent,
In every leaf, a blessing lent.

Beneath the sky so vast and wide,
We sing together, side by side.
In harmony, our voices blend,
In love's pure light, our hearts will mend.

As blossoms dance in gentle breeze,
Our spirits lift, our worries cease.
In sacred circles, joy ignites,
A fragrant whisper in the nights.

O let the petals pave the way,
For every soul to find its sway.
In unity, through trials we bind,
The blossoms of the spirit shine.

The Refuge of the Redeemed

Within the walls of grace we stand,
A shelter built by God's own hand.
In whispers soft, His love we claim,
A haven safe, in His name.

Through storms that rage and darkness creep,
In faith we find the strength to leap.
Each tear we shed, a tale untold,
In arms of mercy, we behold.

Connected hearts in sacred trust,
In truths eternal, rise we must.
For every wound, the light will heal,
In sacred bonds, our spirits feel.

The weary find a place to rest,
In loving arms, we feel so blessed.
With every prayer, a chain we weave,
In unity, we dare believe.

O refuge for the lost we seek,
In humble souls, the brave and weak.
Together bound, we rise anew,
The love of Christ will carry through.

In shadows cast by doubt and fear,
We gather 'round, our hearts sincere.
The refuge made for those redeemed,
In faith's embrace, we are esteemed.

The Prayer of Persistence

In silence deep, we lift our plea,
With every breath, we seek to see.
The path laid out, though frail and thin,
We march in faith, our hearts within.

When trials come, and hope feels lost,
We bear the weight, we count the cost.
Persistent souls in light abide,
With patience strong, our hearts collide.

Through shadows cast and nights so long,
We sing the ancient, sacred song.
Each note a thread, a guiding line,
A testament our spirits shine.

In fervent hearts, the fire burns,
With every step, the world we turn.
Unbroken faith, like rivers flow,
In every prayer, sweet blessings grow.

O let us stand, united here,
With steadfast love, we'll conquer fear.
In prayers of strength, we find our way,
Through trials faced, we shall not sway.

For all that's sought, we shall receive,
In thorns of doubt, we still believe.
With every tear, our spirit's gift,
In fervent prayer, our souls will lift.

Withstanding the Tempest

When tempests rise and waters churn,
In faith's embrace, the heart will learn.
For every storm, a guiding star,
The light of hope will take us far.

In shadows long, we stand as one,
Our praises sung when day is done.
With every gust, our roots run deep,
In holy ground, our spirits keep.

Against the winds, we will not break,
In love's foundation, we awake.
A fortress strong, our hearts align,
In trials faced, the truth will shine.

O let the waves come crashing down,
In unity, we'll wear the crown.
For every trial, our hearts shall climb,
Through winds of change, we seek the sublime.

With steadfast souls, we'll brave the night,
In darkest hours, we find the light.
Together, hand in hand, we stand,
In faith's embrace, a sacred band.

When all is lost, we shall not flee,
For in this storm, we'll find our glee.
Withstanding all, our spirits soar,
Through every tempest, we will roar.

In the Embrace of Eternity

In stillness found, our hearts entwined,
With grace divine, we seek the light.
A path of peace, where love is blind,
In shadows deep, we find what's right.

An endless thread, a tapestry,
Woven with faith, in timeless grace.
Through trials faced, all fear will flee,
As He abides in this holy space.

Eternal bonds, we dare to trust,
In whispers soft, His voice we hear.
With open hearts, as pure as dust,
We journey on, erasing fear.

The stars align, our spirits soar,
In unity, we stand as one.
Love's gentle tide, forevermore,
In His embrace, we are reborn.

So let us walk this sacred way,
With every step, His love to seek.
In night's embrace, we find the day,
In faith we're strong, though hearts may break.

The Whisper of Assurance

In silent nights, a promise lies,
A soothing balm for weary souls.
With open hearts, we hear the cries,
Of grace that heals, and hope consoles.

Beneath the weight of darkened skies,
A whisper comes, so soft and sweet.
In trials fierce, the spirit flies,
With every challenge, we feel complete.

Through stormy seas, the light persists,
Each wave embraces, every trial.
In love's embrace, the heart insists,
To find the peace that makes us smile.

The dawn ignites the shadows' flight,
With every breath, His truth aligns.
A steady hand amid the fright,
In whispered dreams, our spirit shines.

So lift your gaze and trust the way,
For in the dark, the light will bloom.
His voice will guide, come what may,
In hope's embrace, the heart finds room.

Resilient Roots of Righteousness

In fertile ground, our roots will thrive,
With faith that holds through storm and strife.
In righteousness, our spirits strive,
To stand in truth, embracing life.

As trees that bend, yet do not break,
We nurture love, in every deed.
In trials faced, we shall not shake,
For grace provides each heartfelt need.

With branches wide, we reach for grace,
In every heart, compassion sown.
Through every tear, we find our place,
In unity, we are not alone.

The winds may howl, the storms may roar,
Yet in our hearts, the light remains.
We share the gifts, and evermore,
In righteous ways, we break the chains.

So let us grow, and let us shine,
With roots that anchor, deep and strong.
In every moment, sacred sign,
Together we sing a righteous song.

Sacred Echoes of Self

In quiet moments, wisdom calls,
A voice within, so true and clear.
Through sacred echoes, spirit sprawls,
In every heart, we find our cheer.

The journey flows, like rivers wide,
With every step, our truth revealed.
In joy and pain, we will abide,
For in the heart, the love is sealed.

In sacred spaces, we reflect,
The light that dwells in all we see.
With eyes that seek, we will protect,
The essence of our divinity.

Embrace each flaw, for it is grace,
A tapestry of life and soul.
In every tear, we find our place,
Together striving to be whole.

So trust the journey, let it unfold,
In echoes strong, our spirits find.
A sacred truth, a love untold,
In every heart, the light is kind.

Light in the Midst of Trial

In shadows deep, where hope seems lost,
The light of faith, a guiding cost,
Through storms that rage and trials that bind,
A flame of grace, within we find.

With every tear, a promise made,
In darkest nights, our hearts remade,
Through valleys low, we walk the line,
Embraced by love, our souls align.

When burdens weigh and spirits pale,
In whispered prayer, our hearts exhale,
For every struggle, a lesson learned,
In each ascent, our spirits burned.

The dawn will break, the skies will clear,
In suffering's depth, we draw near,
For every trial, a path is shown,
In trials faced, our strength has grown.

So let your heart hold fast to grace,
In every moment, seek His face,
For in the trials, light shall rise,
A beacon bright, beneath the skies.

The Still Small Voice Within

In quiet moments, hearts attune,
A gentle whisper, soft as June,
Truth softly calls in silence deep,
The sacred voice, our souls to keep.

Through chaos loud, its sound remains,
A tender guide to ease our pains,
In solitude, we find our way,
The inner light that will not sway.

Oh, listen close, for wisdom speaks,
In every heart, the spirit seeks,
With every breath, we hear the song,
A melody where we belong.

In trials faced, it offers peace,
A calm assurance, sweet release,
When fears arise, and doubts ensue,
This still small voice will carry you.

Within the soul, a treasure shines,
In every heart, pure love aligns,
Trust the whisper, hold it near,
For in that voice, God's presence is clear.

Standing on Sacred Ground

Where wisdom flows like rivers wide,
We stand in grace, with hearts as guide,
Upon the earth, a hallowed space,
In every breath, we feel His grace.

With every step, a prayer we make,
In nature's hands, our spirits wake,
The sacred soil beneath our feet,
In every challenge, strength we meet.

In gathering storms, the skies may roar,
Yet anchored here, we seek for more,
With open hearts, we feel the sound,
The voice of love, in sacred ground.

Through trials faced, and burdens shared,
In unity, our spirits bared,
We lift each other, side by side,
In sacred trust, we shall abide.

For in this place, His love abounds,
A holy light, in joy surrounds,
Together, on this sacred way,
We rise in faith, come what may.

The Divine Spark of Identity

Within each soul, a flame ignites,
A spark of life that claims our rights,
In every heart, a purpose grand,
The divine touch, by loving hand.

With every breath, a story told,
In shadows cast, our truth unfolds,
We rise as one, to greet the dawn,
In unity, our strength is drawn.

Though paths may diverge and seek their course,
In every heart, a sacred source,
The flame ignites, we claim our pain,
In struggle faced, our truths remain.

As stars that shine in darkest skies,
We find our worth, in love's reprise,
For in our cores, the spirit glows,
A beacon bright, where wisdom flows.

So know your worth, embrace your grace,
In every heart, a sacred place,
For you are known, and you are free,
The divine spark, your legacy.

Milton Keynes UK
Ingram Content Group UK Ltd.
UKHW031321271124
451618UK00007B/162